ans

ˉ

_

I

)n of

itham

r

h Office

STATE LIBRARIAN: Journal of the Circle of State Librarians
Editor: Lewis Foreman
Vol 42   no 1.

Issue No 1 1994

The final issue of *State Librarian* to appear in the long-familiar A4 yellow cover was Vol 39 No 3. Since then each issue of the journal has divided into two components: a monograph on a specific theme published by HMSO, and "News and Views" distributed to members by the CSL, but not available to non-members. We apologise if this has caused any confusion. *State Librarian* appears three times per year, nominally in March, July and November, though from the first issue of 1994 they will be designated as 1/1994; 2/1994; 3/1994 and not by the date as hitherto. Each year's issues, together with the relevant issues of "News and Views" will comprise one volume.

The issues published by HMSO so far under the new arrangements are:

Developing Quality in Libraries (March 1992)
   ISBN 0 11 887537 X

Developing Professionals in Information Work (July/Nov 1992)
   ISBN 0 11 887539 6

Change in Libraries and Information Services (March 1993)
   ISBN 0 11 887542 6

Performance and Potential of Librarians edited by Linda Kerr
   (July 1993) ISBN 0 11 887543 4

Market Testing and After (Nov 1993)
ISBN 0 11 887545 0

All back issues except Nov 1993 (at £7.95) are priced at £6.95 and orders should be placed with HMSO.

ISBN 0 11 887547 7   ISSN 0305–9189

Contents

Contributors

Douglas D'Enno is a translator of long experience having worked at MAFF for many years. He has been Head of MAFF Translation Section since 1979.

Pablo Dubois is Head of Information Systems at the International Coffee Organisation, and was previously Librarian/Research Officer. He is the author of many papers on indexing languages, information management and office automation.

Stephen Latham
Stephen Latham worked at the library of the London School of Economics before joining FCO Library in 1990, working on current awareness and enquiry services. He became Library Systems Manager in 1992, and has written extensively on the application of information technology in Library and Information Services.

Liz MacLachlan is Chair of the Circle of State Librarians, and Information Management Co-ordinator in the DTI. Previously she was the Librarian of the Central Veterinary Laboratory, after posts in the FCO and ODA Libraries.

Tony McSeán is the Librarian of the British Medical Association, and is President of the European Association for Health Information and Libraries. He was formerly with the British Library.

John Scott-Cree is Chief Cataloguer and Systems Librarian in the Department of Environment Library, and before that was in the Home Office Library. He is active in the cataloguing and indexing world and is a member of the Wheatley Committee.

David A Smith is programme manager for the Department of Health's Document and Information Management Strategy. Formerly DH Systems Librarian and a qualified trainer, he has worked on a variety of computer and document management projects in DOE, DH, CCTA and the Civil Service College.

Networking and Libraries: technological innovation and the transformation of information services

Stephen Latham

Library Systems Manager, Foreign & Commonwealth Office

The development of networking technology has transformed the nature and activities of many Library and Information Services (LIS) in recent years. Online searching of remote commercial databases was among the first uses of networking by libraries back in the 1970s. This was later supplemented by access to databases, bulletin boards and E-mail facilities via national and international networks such as JANET and Internet. During the 1980s many libraries developed networks of dumb terminals linked to in-house databases and library management systems. The emergence of powerful PC networks in the late 1980s provided the basis for integrating a wide range of office automation and information resources. This trend has continued in the 1990s, with emphasis on multi-protocol networks and the seamless integration of diverse applications and environments. For the LIS sector these developments have greatly enhanced the quality and range of services which can be offered. The routine work of many staff has altered dramatically, and the whole concept of a Library is being radically redefined within an evolving framework of electronic communication.

This collection of papers brings together a range of insights into the diverse and far reaching impact which networking in its various forms is exerting on the LIS sector: Tony McSeán describes how the BMA Library has come to provide networked access to Medline for thousands of remote medical personnel; Pablo Dubois discusses the use of a Local Area Network to support a variety of information and office automation facilities within a small information oriented organisation; and my own article describes how networking technology has been harnessed to integrate and develop a diverse range of computer systems, supporting the delivery of library and information services to the Foreign & Commonwealth Office, its overseas posts and the Overseas Development Administration.

The increasing strategic importance of networking technology in achieving organisational goals is leading many organisations to define office wide networking strategies. David Smith describes the Office Information System at the Department of Health, and the part which LIS are playing in this. His paper is one of several to focus on the increasing use of networked CD—ROM to deliver services to both library staff and end users. John Scott-Cree from the Department of the Environment Library describes some aspects of an office networking strategy in his own department, and Douglas D'Enno covers the specialised use of a network by the translation service at MAFF. Among the most thought provoking contributions is that of Liz Mac-Lachlan who, as Information Management Coordinator at the Department of Trade and Industry, has moved beyond the traditional library setting altogether. Her paper focuses on the professional challenges and opportunities which networking offers for LIS staff.

There is already a broad literature on the use of networking technology within the LIS sector. However, the current pace of innovation and the potential to exploit this technology means that what we have seen is only the start of a revolution which may ultimately transform the LIS sector beyond all recognition. As diverse organisations set their sights on long term goals within an increasingly electronic information world, the effective use of networking technology has become a key, both to the achievement of those goals and to the whole future of the LIS sector. This collection of papers should provide a current insight into the efforts of a cross section of LIS to stake a claim in an increasingly networked information world of which we are a part.

DIMS Brightens DH: Document and Information Management Strategy at the Department of Health

David A Smith
Document and Information Management Strategy Manager

The Department of Health (DH) currently has an Office Information System (OIS which links most staff on the DH estate together over a Novell Netware based wide area network (WAN). Each person accessing OIS, as the WAN has come to be known, has a 386 or 486 PC and access to wordprocessing and email facilities. WordPerfect 5.1 is the wordprocessing package currently used, and Route400 the email package, allowing OIS users to send and receive ASCII WordPerfect, and binary files (or any combination of these) across the system. Approximately 5,500 users access OIS, and all have access to networked laser printers.

Technical overview: OIS is linked by ethernet Local Area Networks (LANs) within buildings, and between buildings via a router WAN. It provides a basic physical network infrastructure, a server platform of approximately 90 Netware 3.11 servers, standard character-based workstations, location independent access via a standard menu interface, a standard word processing facility, E-mail and access, including terminal emulation, to a number of existing host computers including a Prime minicomputer, Amdahl mainframe, ICL mainframe and various Unix Systems. Users who need task switching, or to use Windows applications, are being transferred to an OIS standard, location independent implementation of Windows 3.1 (OIS/W), after a successful pilot. Approximately 950 OIS users now have OIS/W.

OIS currently provides a limited number of standard applications (Wordperfect 5.1, Route400 E-mail and a bespoke "Staff Location" database). In addition, individual users (or groups of users) have access to a variety of non-standard products including spreadsheets (Lotus 1–2–3, Lotus Symphony, Supercalc, Excel, etc), databases (Dbase, Paradox, Cardbox, Informix, etc). Desk Top Publishing graphics and statistical/financial modelling packages. PC workstations include Compaq and Siemens-Nixdorf 386 and 486 based PCs, with a minimum configuration of 4MB RAM and 40 MB HD, VGA colour screens and network cards. OIS servers (Intel, Compaq, Siemens-Nixdorf) are configured to a standard specification, each including at least a 486 processor, 32MB RAM, 1.2GB of disk storage and DAT tape drive for automatic overnight backup. Each user has access to a nearby network laser printer (HP Laserjet 3 or 4).

LANs within buildings use 10 Base T ethernet transport mechanisms, with 100 Mbit/s Fibre Distributed Data Interface (FDDI) rings linking floors in the buildings serving larger user populations. Links to host computers, including the Department's Prime, use TCP/IP. The WAN backbone consists of high speed leased circuits linking resilient dual operational routers in five main buildings. Other sites are connected by site routers and leased bearers.

Network installation issues: The original business justification for what is one of the largest Whitehall networks, was the transfer of a large part of the DH's business, mainly concerned with the then NHS Management Executive, to Quarry House in Leeds. This move of 1,000 civil servants created an urgent need to ensure that good communications were set up between the London and Leeds communities, and the ability to transfer documents as easily as possible between geographically disparate sections within the same division. Supplemented by video conferencing facilities, OIS was installed in the DH estate over 24 months, which is a very short timescale considering the number of staff to be networked, and the fact that a number of them were in the process of moving to another part of the country.

Document and Information Management Strategy: One consequence of the short installation timescale imposed by the Leeds move was that considerations of the use of OIS as a means of disseminating corporate information were left to later, while the more immediate unstructured document creation and transfer facilities took priority. In 1993 DH's Information Services Directorate (ISD), which encompasses the DH's computer services sections as well as library services and Departmental records, issued a Document and Information Management Strategy (DIMS) paper which was approved by the Departmental Information Strategy Steering Committee. DIMS proposed a number of initiatives to improve the management of information and documents both on OIS and in the Department generally.

Document management Initiative: One of the first issues DIMS addressed arising out of OIS was that of official records. The current policy of the Public Records Office (PRO) is not to accept electronic records, except in exceptional circumstances. Official documents should be stored, in paper format by Departmental Records Managers, and more important ones transferred to the PRO in due course. With the widespread use of OIS, however, DH was faced with an increasing culture of storing important documents across the electronic based system, in email files, wordprocessed files etc, and as a result gaps were appearing in the official records of DH as vital documents failed to be transferred from electronic to paper based systems. To try and address this a Document Management Initiative is underway within DH involving the issuing of guidance and supplemented by a division-by-division rollout of seminars and training. This seeks not to dissuade people from using OIS, but to encourage greater responsibility in carrying out housekeeping tasks, including the transfer of relevant documents to the official paper based record.

The Document Management Initiative is important for two other reasons however. Firstly, the Open Government initiative may see an increased demand for access to official papers by the public and outside bodies. This demand will prove difficult to meet if the papers requested are haphazardly spread out across OIS and cannot be easily retrieved. Secondly, the great increase in the number of documents stored on OIS threatens to give rise to capacity problems on the system. The need to remove important documents to archive (official files) and delete redundant or ephemeral files becomes crucial in ensuring the system is not swamped; this is seen as one of the key objectives of the Document Management Initiative.

Networked Information Services: DIMS proposed a number of ways of reducing the number of documents being stored on the system, and of making greater use of the networking opportunities OIS offered to disseminate information. One of these was the development of information services over the network. These would seek to speed up the amount of routine information distributed across the Department, and to offer a more disk capacity efficient alternative to using purely large scale email distributions.

Staff Location Database: A precedent for this already existed on OIS, as the Department's formerly paper based internal telephone directory, the Staff Location Directory (SLD), had been transferred to OIS and could be accessed using a simple search front end. The data for this was distributed overnight to the file servers that supported the IS user population, and staff accessed this data from a common location on their local file server. By distributing the data in this way, ISD avoided the need for heavy traffic across the WAN accessing one single common point. The total size of data was comparatively small for the SLD; indeed it can be accessed as a TSR running within approximately 32K of RAM.

Press Index Service: The first information service identified for this "treatment" was the daily Press Summary and DH Press Notices issued daily by the Department's Information Division. A project was set up with the objectives of providing all DH staff with daily access to two files: one of the press headlines of interest to the DH, and the other the full text of DH Press Releases. This was achieved by having the two files prepared by Information Division, who receive the press Summary electronically from an external source and who hold their Press Releases electronically anyway. The actual files contain one week's coverage of Press Summaries and Press Notices, and can be easily scrolled through using WordPerfect. Both files are loaded simultaneously into WordPerfect, and the user can switch between the two, scrolling or using the FIND function to search each file. Access to the service is via an INFORMATION option on the top level OIS menu for DOS users, or a Press Index Service icon within an INFORMATION group for Windows users.

Distribution of the data is made from a central point on the network to predefined locations on Novell file servers offering shared access to users logged into these. Effects on the network of this short burst of traffic have been negligible, but all such DIMS proposals as these are first tested out on a reference network which seeks to emulate the true OIS network, but under carefully monitored conditions. This procedure helps to overcome potential technical problems that could cause widespread chaos if changes to the WAN were rolled out untested.

As with all the planned DIMS related information services, cash releasing benefits were a virtual prerequisite for acceptance of the Press Index Service business case. In this case a saving of 0.5 of an AO (no longer required for the manual distribution) and approximately

£15,000 in the print budget were identified. A better informed staff may be a desirable thing to achieve in the eyes of the library/ information services community, but money talks in Finance Division. The rollout of this service is scheduled for completion by the end of October 1994 to all OIS users.

Hansard Summary Service: A PRINCE methodology was employed to run this project, in common with most ISD run projects. In order to get the fullest utility from this process, in terms of technical design and quality assurance, ISD has sought to "boiler plate" DIMS projects as much as possible. This should ensure that experience gained from past DIMS projects is brought to bear in future ones. In the case of the Press Index Service project, the same technical design will be used to produce the next DIMS project, the daily *Hansard* summary. This will, again, be two WordPerfect files updated daily, distributed to the OIS user population by the same means as the Press Index Service. In the case of the *Hansard* summary the two files will list debates and POS of relevance to DH from the most recent Hansard; one file will cover House of Commons Hansard, the other Lords.

The cash releasing saving for this project will, however, different from Press Index. Annually DH spends approximately £85,000 on daily *Hansard* subscriptions, it is estimated that this figure can be reduced by £15,000 in the first year of operation of the service by substituting the hardcopy with the OIS facility. The *Hansard* summary will be drawn up by the Library and parliamentary branch, and the Library service will be responsible for the provision of hardcopies of the *Hansard* items requested from the summary. The ability to provide on demand hardcopy over OIS is a further development that is desirable for both the Press and *Hansard* services, but the issues involved in storing and transmitting scanned images, to say nothing of copyright, still need to be addressed.

Networked CD-ROMs: A different type of facility proposed by DIMS, and one in which the OIS users are interested, is end user access to networked CD-ROM facilities. The existing use of CD-ROM within DH had, up to mid 1993, been confined to public access to CD-ROM workstations located in DH libraries. Selection and payment for CD-ROM products was made by the library service, and searching was carried out predominantly by trained library staff. The planned implementation of access to networked CD-ROM facilities, under DIMS, envisaged DH staff accessing the CD-ROM products directly themselves from their own workstations located on their desks.

A trial has been initiated to examine the effect and costs of providing end user access to CD-ROM products, with a view to a full departmental rollout in the light of the experience gathered from the pilot. The product selected for this trial was HMSO's *Civil Service Yearbook* on CD-ROM, as this would allow the library to substitute a number of retention copies held by staff with the networked CD-ROM version.

A total of 20 users are involved in the trial, and were selected from a list of those currently receiving a retention copy of the *Civil Service Year Book*. The networked CD-ROM cost £150.00 for a five user licence (five concurrent users), but this enabled the library to save approximately £400.00 in hardcopy subscriptions. Although small in the context of this trial, the cash releasing saving is important as it forms a crucial element in drawing up an eventual business case for Departmental-wide rollout. The library purchases a significant number of reference publications for retention by staff which, if replaced by the equivalent publication on CD-ROM, could offer significant overall savings as well as added functionality over the hardcopy.

The ability to demonstrate cash releasing savings, or "crunchy" savings as they are sometimes called, is now becoming increasingly important in justifying information projects. The hard economic realities of current life mean that benefits such as "better informed" users are perceived as "squidgy" benefits with no cash savings *directly* attributable to them. This is not to say that these are not legitimate benefits, but a greater emphasis is being put on showing tangible benefits, expressed in staff or budgets saved, derived from new information sources.

So far the pilot has been running for four months and a number of technical issues have arisen, two of which are worthy of note. The first is that the release of CD-NET software we are currently using, though fairly stable when working in a purely DOS environment, is inherently unstable within Windows causing individual PCs to hang through lack of available memory. At present only a small proportion of the users in the trial are using Windows to access the network, but this number is rapidly increasing and it is likely that eventually all DH staff will use Windows as their main desktop on the PC. This problem can be overcome by purchasing the newer release of CD-NET software, but is worth bearing in mind for those finding problems in migrating from purely DOS to Windows.

Another point has been that the *Civil Service Year Book* CD-ROM contains the search software on the disk itself. This has the advantage of avoiding the need to install the information retrieval software onto the PCs of all potential users of the CD-ROM, but does mean that additional traffic has to be carried over the Novell backbone of OIS as

.exe files are downloaded onto logical drives. Technically this can be overcome, but the potential need for the network to be able to transfer additional executable files for some networked CD-ROM products will affect the topography of the technical solution proposed to enable *all* users on the OIS network to potentially access networked CD-ROM facilities. Other CD-ROM titles, such as JUSTIS or PolTox (prior to its transfer to Silver Platter) require the retrieval software to be installed on the workstation which, although easing the burden of network traffic, creates support issues concerned with distributing, installing and upgrading the software—not easy on a 5000 user WAN.

A number of non-technical issues still need to be resolved. How do we charge users who want access to "specialist" CD-ROMS for which they are willing to pay, but which would not be offered to all users? What networked CD-ROM products should new users to the network get as "standard", if any? How are the licensing and copyright issues to be dealt with, particularly if a proposed topography involves the use of multiple copies of a CD-ROM product in order to adequately service the whole of the DH estate? Can the internal DH helpdesk support a potential population of 5,000 end users? Should the library? All of these issues may have to be taken into consideration in assessing the overall "crunchy" savings of offering end user access to CD-ROM products over a LAN.

It is unlikely that any final decisions concerning wide scale end user access to networked CD-ROM facilities will take place until the end of 1994. Until then further work needs to be done, not only on the technical problems of offerig this service, to convince the people holding the purse strings that the squidgy benefits of end users CD-ROM searching on a LAN are backed up by suitable crunchy savings.

Distribution of Business: The final service for which rollout is expected in 1994 is the DH Distribution of Business. This is DH's internal directory of who does what in the Department; OGDS will have similar publications carrying out the same function. Using the same technology as was used for the SLD, the Distribution of business (DOB) will be made available to users in the autumn, on a fully free text search basis. One problem that did face ISD in developing this as an electronic service, was incorporating the user demand for a thesaurus to help navigate round parts of the Department's work unfamiliar to most staff. Coincidentally an 18,000 term Departmental Standard Thesaurus, also one of the DIMS recommendations, was completed in February and it was decided to interface this with the DOB.

The result has been a thesaurus "option" which can be turned on or off when using the DOB, but which can otherwise be completely transparent to the user. This allows the user to enter a non-preferred term, but to automatically retrieve sections that are described using the preferred term linked to it. Where a term is retrieved through the thesaurus it is highlighted in red to alert the user; terms located through a free text search are highlighted in grey. The thesaurus is also useful in "translating" abbreviations that are used in describing the work of the Department. The thesaurus is run against the text of the DOB each day, and any terms in the thesaurus not linked to text in the DOB are removed. The result is that users search a "sub-thesaurus", which contains terms that will always result in a retrieved section(s) if entered.

There are other DIMS projects in the "pipeline" for 1995/6, and these include end user searching of the Staff Code, provision of electronic Room Notices, and the ability of all 5,000 users to have end user access to the Library's OPAC and other library services, (eg the full text of Departmental circulars). OIS has thrown up a lot of opportunities to utilise IT in the DH: DH librarians and information scientists are making sure that the Information component is not forgotten when developing IT networks.

DAWSON ON-LINE SERVICES

BOOKS

The Importance of Wide Area Networks for the Future Development of Government Information and Library Services

Liz MacLachlan

Information Management Co-ordinator, Department of Trade & Industry

Local Area Networks (LANs) can bring very large benefits in improving both the communication within a library and the access to expensive resources such as the catalogue, CD-ROMs and external databases. Those who have used LANs are quickly convinced that they are an essential tool to efficient operation. However, I believe that LANs are only the first stage in an effective information and library service. LANs allow information staff to communicate with others on the network (ie with each other). To communicate with the customers you need more, you need a Wide Area Network or WAN.

WANs can be of several kinds, but the most common is a network of LANs, allowing different groups to communicate with each other. They have been around in government for a long time. For example, by 1983 MAFF had linked the minicomputers (mostly PRIMEs) based in the regional HQS and laboratories throughout the country to the computer centre in Guildford and to each other. Mostly used for E-Mail, the MAFF WAN also allowed access to 60-odd STATUS databases and to departmental systems, so long as the searcher had the appropriate rights. Most departments have had networks connecting at least those parts with a common interest and a need to communicate. In recent years two factors have combined to speed up this process, decentralisation and office systems.

Departments which have traditionally had a widespread regional network have evolved their own methods of communication. Frequently the communication has been star shaped, between the centre and the local office, but with little traffic between local offices. The push to move out of central London in the latter half of the 1980s meant that sections which used to be side by side, often in the same building might now be two hours by fast train apart. The obvious answer was electronic communication, and departments such as Health and Employment, which have had substantial decentralisation programmes, have invested heavily in networks to keep themselves connected. Decentralisation of function, such as local personnel management, is now having a similar effect.

At the same time the technology of office systems has begun to mature, and group working seems to offer further opportunities to increase efficiency. Office systems typically consist of a number of interlocking facilities using a common interface which can be accessed from a single PC. In addition to the standard products (word processing, spreadsheet, database) they include electronic diary, shared electronic filing system, E-Mail and access to X400 networks. Telex and fax can be included and most systems also have some sort of shared bulletin board area which can be used for a variety of purposes. LANs connect the PCs of people in the same workgroup, and a WAN links the LANs, both to each other and to the outside world. Most departments have systems either installed or in development.

Office systems allow for far greater access to information through-out the organisation, and the capacity to move it around faster. For information professionals they are both a threat and an opportunity. As users become more familiar with networks, and more aware of external information sources, so many of them will wish to do their own on-line searching and buy their own CD-ROMs. With the world's information available through the INTERNET what need is there for librarians?

And yet I believe that office systems provide the opportunity for librarians to break out of the library, and to make a real impact on the way that information is managed within their departments. Large IT projects, both outside and inside government, have a poor track record. According to different sources between 45 and 95 per cent fail to deliver all the benefits expected of them. One of the reasons for this is that, even when the technical issues are resolved, systems do not give the user something that he finds useful.[1] By focusing on the *content* not the delivery mechanism, librarians can make the differ-ence. There are three main areas where information professionals can have most impact:

- making available existing information sources such as the library's own catalogue;

17

- helping users access CD-ROMs and commercial databases;

- developing new services to help users sift through the mountains of irrelevance which pass across their desks for the core of what they need to know in a form they can use directly.

The first and most obvious candidate for putting onto a WAN is the library catalogue. It is likely to be in electronic form already, and it is the key to a major information resource, the library collections. An important side effect is an immediate increase in visibility for the library service. When the Department for Education mounted its DYNIX catalogue over the office network, it saw a marked increase in business. Others have had less success. In theory, vets from Lasswade to Starcross had access to the Central Veterinary Laboratory library catalogue and database of periodical articles. In fact, apart from a few enthusiasts, few ever used it. Partly this was due to lack of terminals, partly to the unfriendliness and difficulty of using the catalogue itself.

The purpose of the catalogue is to help the user find what he is looking for. Users want to know if the library has information:

- on a particular subject;

- by a particular author;

- with a particular title.

Authors and titles are likely to be random, and subjects imprecise. Most users find the books they want by serendipity, wandering along the shelves until they find the right section rather than by using the catalogue or, absolute last resort, asking the librarians.

On a WAN the librarians are not there to ask. The catalogue must be redesigned to welcome and support the end user. Instructions for searching must be clear, and involve choosing from menus or the minimum number of keystrokes, with short cuts for the more experienced. The user must be able to enter a term and get an answer. The language must be free from jargon. Entry of a name must take him to an alphabetical list, not a "number of hits = 0" message. Subject searching must be supported by at least some of the following: synonym control, a structured thesaurus, fuzzy matching or relevance ranking. The user must be able to browse, by author, subject or series. When the user finds the items he wants the records must be presented in the way he wants. Full citations of the sort

iv, 234, xx, col.ill., 5 plts, Bib, Index

are out. Contents listings on request are in. The user must be able to download in the form he wants, to be incorporated directly into a word processor or database. And of course he must be able to locate the item, check its availability, order a loan or photocopy, reserve and renew, all remotely from his desk.

End user access to commercial databases has been slow in government. Apart from specialised areas, such as defence or some research labs, users have either not known what is available or have believed online to be some sort of arcane mystery practised by initiates speaking strange tongues. They have also been put off by the logistical problems in getting connected and by the fear of uncontrollable, large bills. As users become accustomed to communicating with each other over LANs, and to having very much greater access to local databases, their awareness of and desire for commercial sources will increase. This is a trend which should be encouraged, to the point of force if necessary. When users realise what is available on commercial databases they want it, lots of it. In particular they want tailored services to tell them what is important in their world. Libraries will not be able to cope with the demand, nor will they be able to afford to pay for it from shrinking budgets. Only by devolving out the work, and the costs, to the users themselves can the situation be sensibly managed.

Librarians need not fear that they will become redundant. More sophisticated users will still seek professional help for more complex searches on unusual databases. A more important role, however, will be to help the end user to decide what online sources are most relevant to his particular needs. A recent search for the top 100 companies on three different databases produced three different answers. No surprise for librarians, but users need to understand what they are getting. A guide, over the office system, to what information is available on which system, how to get access (including through the library) and assesses the "quality" of the data, will be an essential tool. Quality is a major issue, users must feel assured that they can rely on the information they retrieve. The setting up of the new Centre for Information Quality Management[2], jointly promoted by the Library Association and UKOLUG as a clearing house for database quality issues is a welcome development.

Librarians should also advise on sources of training, and facilitate internal user-group type activity. They should evaluate systems such as COMMINCATOR or INFORMATION PARTNER, which are designed to help the naive user search effectively and control costs. They need to iron out the technical difficulties in getting online, or in networking CD-ROMs, understanding the technical issues and translating between the users and the computer people. They should also manage all licence arrangements, and monitor usage to get the best deal for the organisation from the suppliers.

E-Mail will become the primary communication and delivery mechanism around the departments, and between the library and its users. It is vital that E-Mail formats make processes easy. Loan or renewal requests should click up from the catalogue, enquiry requests should include all the information needed such as deadlines, what the information is needed for and the format it is wanted in. SDIs should be run, reformatted and mailed automatically.

Well known to network users (and hackers!) bulletin boards offer the library the opportunity to advertise itself and its products. Current awareness lists can be posted on the bulletin board for everyone to see, saving paper and reproduction costs. Special user groups allow a more targeted approach. Guidance on the use of systems, advice on sources, "hot topics", library news bulletins can all be mounted quickly and easily, and updated frequently. Bulletin boards are best for short, current, newsy information. Anything more substantial, where choices are required or a life longer than a few weeks is expected, needs a different approach, probably a database.

Librarians should not restrict themselves to traditional library-type information. Our skills in manipulating unstructured text-based systems are needed in the design and indexing of electronic departmental information sources such as notices, manuals, instructions and guides. Hypertext offers a possible way forward, and here the library profession is in the lead. There are obvious and substantial opportunities for saving, in paper, reproduction, distribution. Filing time can be costed and saved. More difficult to estimate are the results of poor decisions based on inaccurate information. By taking the lead in developing systems to exploit departmental information sources, and enabling these savings to take place, librarians can both become more visible and have an objective measure of their value.

Raising the profile also means taking a stand on standards. Working in a shared environment is very different from working as a stand-alone. It increases the speed and range of communication, saves time in preparing documents, and allows for sharing of expensive resources like CD-ROMs or internal databases. However, it also brings the capacity for chaos. Without agreed standards and procedures for the information itself, effective sharing cannot take place. Not only will benefits not be realised but there is a danger that information might be lost. Standards do not form themselves, they have to be agreed by people who have, in the past, had little need to understand each other's work. One man's vacuum cleaner is another man's Hoover, one woman's M&S is another's Marks and Spencer plc.

A database, developed by and for a single user, will often contain information which overlaps with another developed by someone else in another section. Yet the two cannot be merged because the data structure is different and different conventions have been adopted for input. The effort of maintaining a database, even a simple name and address contacts list, is considerable. If it is not done regularly the data will rapidly decay. At best this reduces the usefulness of the database, at worst it could lead to embarrassment such as where mailshots are sent to long deceased companies, or worse still individuals. With personal data poor maintenance runs the risk of infringement of the Data Protection Act.

Librarians are well placed to take a lead on standards. They know how to store and retrieve information. They can advise on the structures of local databases and on data sources, both for initial population and up-dating. Where a suitable commercial database exists a local database may not be needed. Librarians can identify where relevant standards already exist, help achieve consensus in devising new standards for data input, advise on indexing and emphasise the importance of consistency. As they cut horizontally across their departments librarians are aware of similar needs, so can identify more opportunities for sharing.

The new service which will make the most impact is an Executive Information System. Users do not want more information, indeed they have too much at the moment. What they want is reliable, timely, accurate information in a form they can use directly; something that will clear the paper off their desks and give them confidence that they have all the essentials. This is where librarians, in government as everywhere, can make the most impact on the effectiveness of their organisations. EIS systems exist, and are concentrated mainly on supplying management, particularly financial information. This is only one small part of what senior managers need to know to keep businesses, as well as departments of state, on track. Jan Wyllie has written about information refineries:

> "Refining information is a socio-technological process which enables intelligent human beings to extract and organize systematically the key items of knowledge kept in any given choice of information sources . . The result of the refining process should be to bring about better, more informed decisions by intelligent decision makers."[3]

Drawing on all the capacity of technology it is still down to "intelligent human beings" to recognise the key facts, trends, snippets of information and to turn them into corporate intelligence. Librarians, with their knowledge of the information people need to do their jobs, the sources to find it and the technological skills to exploit it are ideally placed to become the information refiners in their organisations. Information audits and needs analyses are the techniques which will define the requirement. Libraries, actual or virtual, house the raw material. Office systems provide the delivery mechanism. The spark to unite these into an effective tool is a willingness on the part of librarians to become true information professionals, to get their hands dirty, to take decisions about the information they are handling, and the weight to give it in the decision making process. If we can do that, then we really have broken out of the library. We can prove our value to the organisation, and our future role is secure.

References

1. KPMG Peat Marwick: *Information for strategic management: a survey of leading companies.* KPMG Peat Marwick, 1990.
2. Centre for Information Quality Management. c/o Chris Armstrong, Information Automation Limited, Penbryn, Bronant, Aberystwyth SY23 4TJ. Tel/Fax: 097 421 441.
3. WYLLIE, J: "The need for business information refineries". *Aslib proceedings* 45(4) 1993, 97–102.

The BMA Library's Micro-Host Service: making Medline an unmediated success

Tony McSeán

Librarian, British Medical Association

As working librarians, we are concerned with compiling the best range of data resources for our users and presenting them in a way they will find convenient. Today, our lives have been complicated by the need to decide which range of technologies best matches our users' needs and the nature and resources of our library. Medical librarians have the advantage of operating in a particularly well-defined subject field. The boundaries are clear, the literature is well-established and well-organised and we are served by two outstanding databases—Medline and EMBase. This paper recounts how one group of librarians has tried to make an entirely conventional electronic source available to our users in a way that will, above all, encourage them to use it to the full to benefit their patients.

The Context: In an age of increasing diversity in electronic information products, there is no longer a single "right answer" for every library (or even every medical library). Each library has to plan its services to match its users' requirements. The British Medical Association Library (BMAL) is an unusual library. It is the UK's second-largest medical library and uses the most modern technology to offer medical library and information services to members throughout the world. We are a library for the working doctor, concentrating on current clinical practice, on medical information systems and on ethics.

By many standards, the BMA is not a large Library: 21 staff, including 12 professional librarians; 1,200 current serials; 2,400 medical videos and films. But we are both busy and facing a substantial increase in demand for our services (Figure 1).

Expansion of Services

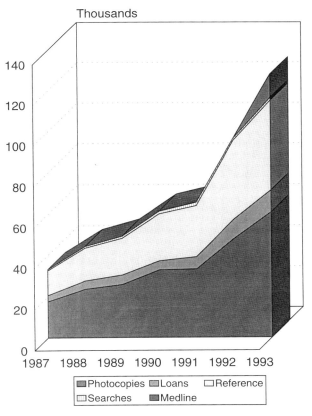

Figure 1

In 1993 we dealt with 44,000 reference enquiries, loaned 10,500 books and videos and supplied 61,000 photocopied citations. So far, a conventional story, but in practice we are an idiosyncratic library. Our main job is to provide members with access to published clinical information, in a way they find most convenient. That last phrase is crucial: our members are spread throughout the UK and for all but a few *the way they find most convenient* will not be by visiting the Reading Room in BMA House.

We have adopted two strategies to make our collections accessible:

> *Reaching Out*: The BMAL's post and telephone services have been progressively supplemented by computer terminals, electronic mail, fax and (now) by fully networked information services.
>
> *Institutional Membership*: One of the most significant developments in BMAL history was the setting up in 1965 of the Library's Institutional Membership scheme. This opens up the library to other institutions which for a small annual subscription, can enjoy more or less the same privilege as a personal member. As budgets have tightened in recent years, this scheme has grown in popularity and there are now nearly 600 libraries using us as a back-up.

A Business-Like Library: BMAL is extremely unexpected in that there is virtually no "captive" user population. Most libraries have a group of people for whom they are the natural information resource: students and staff of the college, ministry staff, etc. We have no such group. Only 2% of all BMA Library activity is generated by users visiting the reading room. The main consequence of this "free-floating" existence is that in planning and operating our services we operate much more like a small business than a conventional library:

> We have to find the significant gaps between our members' information needs and our services.
>
> We have to make sure that our members are aware that they have an information gap.
>
> We have to be aware of our own cost structure—aware of what we can do well and cost-effectively, and aware of the type of service where we cannot compete and should avoid.
>
> Finally, we have to structure, price, market and sell our services to a busy and geographically widespread population of potential users.

If we merely sat back and waited for users to arrive, we would find ourselves without a role and eventually we would close. The BMA is very committed to its Library[1] but we represent a huge and continuing investment of members' money and we need to continue to provide good value for money if we are to continue to justify that investment.

Planning A New Service: In the autumn of 1991, as we started planning for 1992, the Library was healthy and stable. Demand for our services was rising quickly but at a manageable level, with rising revenue funding almost all of the growth. Our main "product lines" of photocopies, loans and reference services were well-regarded and market leaders. As every businessman knows this is the time to innovate: finance available, credibility with customers, good staff morale. We realised that our priority was political—to be seen to be providing a modern, high-value service directly to our personal members. It was obvious that we should be looking at networked information services, probably in the area of information retrieval by end-users using user-friendly search software then becoming available.

The time seemed to be right, with more of the medical profession in the UK using computers than almost anywhere in the world.[2] Original research in March 1993[3] based on a random sample of 367 BMA members has since confirmed our intuitive judgement; with 71% of a random sample of BMA members using computers (Figure 2), of which

UK Doctors' Use of PCs

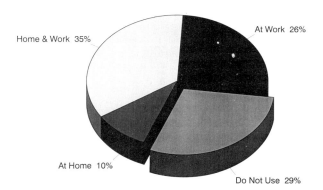

Figure 2

30% have modems. 43% of doctors rated themselves as at least reasonably competent in their use of computers (Figure 3). In relation

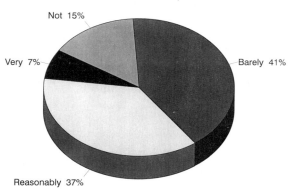

Figure 3

to this paper, the most interesting result from the survey was the ranking which merged when doctors were asked which types of information they would access via networked services. As Figure 4

Doctors' Likely Use of Networked Services

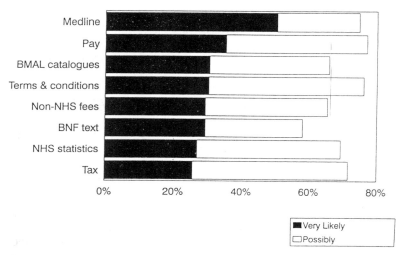

Figure 4

shows, Medline services received the highest rating—above pay and allowances.

In developing networked information services, the UK academic community had already shown the way, first with its universal implementation of the information Joint Academic Network (JANET) network, and more recently with the early phases of the National Datasets Policy.[4] While the pioneering Institute for Scientific Information files were still being made available on JANET, at the BMA we were thinking hard about how we might learn from this experience. It was fortuitous, then, that the Datasets team should start considering medicine, and specifically Medline, as their next subject area. Just when we had decided to contact the National Datasets team to ask if we might become involved, they telephoned the BMA and asked if we were willing to form a Medline consortium, mounting Medline at Bath University on JANET. They offered technical expertise, running costs and project leadership. We had unrivalled access to the UK's medical profession, practical experience of Medline, and were willing to contribute towards the set-up costs. The BMA's leaders were convinced that direct information services would be a worthwhile addition to membership services—so money was available.

Like so many promising alliances, it was not to be for several substantial reasons. For both the national datasets team and BMAL, Plan A was not viable and we both had to reactivate alternative ideas. At this stage it was possible that the respective Plan B would be the same, but by no means inevitable. Plan B for the datasets team was clear: Elsevier was keen for their EMBase file be made available to UK academics, and although there was some keenly fought negotiation it was not long before EMBase was neatly slotted into Medline's place in the programme.

BMAL's options were by no means so neat and clear cut, and embraced a number of technological, professional and operational considerations:

> Do Nothing: We were under no pressure to produce a new service and could have just dropped the idea.

> Virtual Network Online: Discussions were opened with a prominent online host about the possibility of their providing our members with a virtual private network. This would operate as part of their mainstream information retrieval service, but to holders of BMA network identities, it would appear to be a private BMA-only service with customised features. Payment would be either by a single fixed subscription or a cost-per-user fee structure.

EMBase over JANET: A simple option—to cooperate with the datasets team as before and buy into their EMBase service.

PlusNet2: The most radical option was to buy our own copy of Medline and to operate a micro-host service for members using the CD-Plus PlusNet2 system: a proprietary search, retrieval and communications system suitable for non-professional users; running on a PC-based file server, 7.2 gigabytes of magnetic disc drives, plus other equipment described below. The database is a complete copy of Medline, held and searched on hard disc and updated via DAT.

Decision Making: We were very depressed at the failure of the Medline and JANET scheme. So depressed, in fact, that we spent a week telling each other we were going to take the *Do Nothing* option and go back to what we knew was successful. But if we had done that we would have missed an important opportunity, and who can tell when the next one would arise. So, we turned our backs on inaction.

The *Virtual Network* scheme was attractive: it was innovatory; it did not pose us with any particular technical problems; it would be an exclusive arrangement. In the end the idea fell for two reasons:

We found it hard to believe that our chosen host could offer us a completely flat-rate deal, accepting all the financial risks that the service might attract high levels of usage.

They seemed enthusiastic whenever we spoke to them, but their follow-through was less impressive. When you are pioneering in the smallest degree in information technology, it is Priority One to have your system supplier at least as eager for success as you are yourself.

EMBase over JANET was attractive because it was certain to work and we knew we could work well with the others involved. It suffered from EMBase's lower recognition factor amongst BMA members. This is casting no aspersions on the quality, coverage or probity of EMBase. It was just that if we had chosen this option, we would have had to market EMBase to members, on top of all the other elements in the new service.

PlusNet2 had a lot of things running in its favour. It put Medline back at the heart of the project. It could be made exclusive to the BMA, at least for a time. Intensely annoying though it was at the time, the failure of the Medline/JANET deal and the emergence of the EMBase option introduced the opportunity for an exclusive service for our members, and the chance to develop an information service that is in many ways a world's first. The technology was at that ideal stage of development where (a) it was still exciting and innovatory; but (b) we could phone up trustworthy friends in America and check if it really worked. It was also technology which put the system under our own control. CD-Plus were eager to make the sale, the first PlusNet2 outside North America and the first for an application of this type. We were confident of getting at least base-line support.

So we chose to buy PlusNet2. We have implemented a major information retrieval system that makes the major medical sciences database available to our members 24 hours a day, every day of the year. The configuration will, we estimate support about 5,000 registered users. We believe it is the first time that a professional association has provided a service of this type as a free benefit of membership.

Networking: The concept of networking is at the heart of this whole scheme. The Library is networked, using Novell Netware and ethernet, to provide staff and users (including BMA and *British Medical Journal* colleagues) with a range of information resources, and with the ability to send electronic mail messages. The Library acts as the BMA's gateway for electronic mail, and its network implementation will form the model for networking elsewhere in the organisation. Figure 5

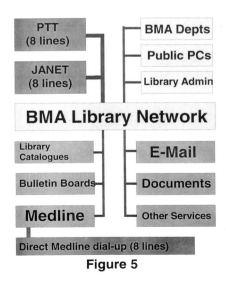

Figure 5

illustrates the network and shows how the 24 lines into the Medline file server are divided into three groups of eight:

> Direct dial into the Medline system, using any hardware/ software combination that can emulate a VT100 terminal. A 386 disc-less PC sits on each of the eight direct lines and acts as a front-end to Medline.

> Dial in access to the Library network, again using VT100 emulation. Users are presented with the Medline service as one of the network options, as a password-protected menu item.

> Access to the Library network via the JANET (Internet) link, with VT200 emulation as the minimum option, and again getting through to Medline via the network menu.

The Service Takes Off: There were two anxieties in the run up to the launch of the new service: *either* members' take-up would be pitifully small, leaving the Library's credibility in tatters with BMA management; *or* we would be overwhelmed by demand and unable to provide user support—with much the same result. In the event, neither happened—although we came close to the latter on occasions.

The service was launched in June 1993, and the public target was 1,000 registered users by the end of the year. As Figure 6 shows, the target was met in 6 weeks and but for a serious flu epidemic would have been doubled by December. The number of members using the system should comfortably exceed 3,000 by the end of 1994, and it has been an exceptional success for the Library both professionally and from the public relations point of view.

Introducing such an enormous number of mostly naive users to dial-up online searching put substantial strains on both help desk and administrative resources. In the event, the delayed delivery of software that doubled the length of the pilot phase was a hidden blessing, because it enabled us to fine tune the documentation. When they sign up for the system, members receive a pack giving the information they need to set up their systems, log on, carry out simple author and subject searches and download the search results to disc or printer. The pack includes modem and software settings, a trouble-shooting guide, some background on Medline and information on document delivery services.

Registered Medline Users

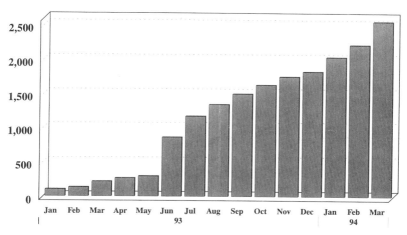

Figure 6

To date, this approach has been reasonably successful. Most of our members have had a sensible appreciation of the nature of the service and of the amount of resources we have to support it. We do get *It doesn't work* phone calls, but the small proportion is growing smaller as the documentation is continually refined.

Limits to Effectiveness: Although it may sound melodramatic, when you deal in medical information people's health and even lives can be at stake, and we have a professional obligation to our members to point out the limitations of the online search process. Online searching is a seductive business and it would be very easy for a doctor to be left with the impression that his or her search had identified all there was to know about a particular subject. The reality is more likely to be that they have located perhaps only one third as much as a professional searcher would have found, which might only be 80% of what the database contained, which in turn might be only half of what has been published, or 15% of the total available information. Given the vagaries of retrieval software, it is highly unlikely to be a random and representative 15%. On top of that, there is the temptation to skim through the abstract and not read the actual paper. This is hardly a basis for informed decision-making on patient care, and may even be worse than no literature search at all. Therefore, all our documentation *and* our normal sign-on screen gives a warning about these dangers.

Introducing the free Medline service was a considerable risk, but one which has paid off handsomely in providing an effective and appropriate service for members. It has proved an enormously effective means of promoting the library's standing within the BMA, and of making the senior management and senior elected officers aware that information and library services are an important component in a professional organisation's repertoire. There is clearly a substantial demand for access to networked information services, and we are taking further steps to meet that by expanding our network and by replacing an ageing cataloguing system with a modern, integrated information management system. By combining this with electronic mail, (and fax, in years to come) we will be in a position to deliver information and library services directly to virtually all our members. How we cope with the resulting expansion in demand is merely next year's problem.

References

1. British Medical Association: *Annual report of council 1993*. BMA, 1993.
2. Information Management Group: *IM&T strategy: an overview*. Leeds, National Health Service Management Executive Information Management group, 1992.
3. British Medical Association Economic Research Unit: Unpublished report on doctors' usage of computers.
4. Law, D G: 'The development of a national datasets policy'. In: *Information transfer: new age—new ways*, edited by Suzanne Bakker and Monique Cleland. Proceedings of the Third European Conference of Medical Libraries). Dordrecht, Kluwer, 1993.

Integration and Development Through Networking: a case study from the Foreign & Commonwealth Office Library

Stephen Latham

Foreign & Commonwealth Office, London

During the 1980s the Foreign & Commonwealth Office (FCO) Library developed a range of information systems and office automation facilities. While some networking was in use to link different library sites there was no overall integration of the various components of the system. In March 1991 a token ring LAN running Novell Netware 386 was installed in the then Cornwall House Library to provide each member of staff with desktop access to the complete range of existing information resources and the tools for exploiting them. The success of the initiative meant that when Cornwall House closed and the libraries amalgamated in the FCO main building, the LAN was extended and upgraded, and now forms a stable and flexible platform on which to develop library systems in the future. The new technology has transformed both working practices, and the ease and sophistication with which library staff can deliver services to the FCO and its overseas posts.

The various systems developed within the library during the 1980s were designed to support specific areas of activity. There were three discrete components to these systems:

- periodicals management;
- stand alone PCs;
- library housekeeping and text retrieval.

In common with many government libraries the first IT development was the introduction of Blackwell's ISIS system (formerly known as Pearl) to manage ordering and circulation of periodicals. This application ran under the MUMPS environment and was mounted on a Plessey mini computer. Library staff had access to ISIS for managing orders and for reference purposes through a number of dedicated dumb terminals supporting VT100 emulation over serial lines.

A variety of stand alone PCs were introduced to support DOS based word processing, spreadsheet packages and small text based database packages. Several PCs ran communications software to access external online hosts through local modems, and a number of stand alone CD-ROM workstations were set up.

An IBM 9370 was installed to support the integrated library management system DOBIS/LIBIS and the text retrieval system STAIRS running under the proprietary VSE/CICS/VTAM environment. DOBIS was used for all housekeeping activities apart from periodicals management and STAIRS was used to support five in-house databases which had outgrown PC based packages. Library staff accessed the system using a mixture of proprietary dumb terminals and PCs running 3270 emulation software to emulate dumb terminals. Networking to remote FCO and Overseas Development Administration (ODA) Library sites used SDLC links across BT Kilostream lines. In the case of ODA Library the SDLC link was mapped onto an Ethernet LAN through a remote gateway.

Figure 1 is a simplified representation of the fragmented systems in use within the library before the introduction of the LAN. While each of these various systems and applications met the specific needs for which they were installed, they did not function collectively to form a cohesive information system for the library. With increasing reliance on electronic sources of information and a growing requirement to package and present information in customised formats, the fragmented structure of the existing systems constrained the library in various ways (see Fig 1).

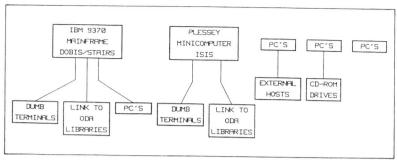

Figure 1: Fragmented Systems

Competing demands for system resources: There were competing demands by library staff for limited system resources. The PCs used for online searching were under great demand with staff having to wait until a PC was free to carry out a search. Word processing and spreadsheet facilities were not universally available and access to DOBIS, STAIRS and ISIS was constrained by the number and location of terminals for these applications. High quality laser printers were not fully utilised because they were dedicated to individual PCs and correspondence was often produced on lower quality printers.

Presentation of information: Facilities for editing data downloaded from various databases were limited. Records from the library catalogue and other databases could only be downloaded from DOBIS and STAIRS to one of a limited number of PCs supporting 3270 emulation. Online and CD-ROM searches tended to be presented to users in their raw format; editing searches meant either using word processing facilities on the CD-ROM or online workstations which were in demand for searching, or downloading the search to a floppy disk and transferring it to a PC which was not in demand. Difficulties arose in transferring files between PCs with incompatible floppy disk drives.

These various constraints arising from the fragmentary structure of the systems in use meant that there was considerable scope for integration through the use of networking technology.

In March 1991 a token ring LAN running Novell Netware 386 was introduced at the main FCO Library site. Existing PCs were fitted with network interface cards to become LAN workstations. These were supplemented by additional low cost PC workstations and an IBM PS2 Model 80 with 8MB RAM and 650MB of disk space acting as a file server. Office automation packages which had been used on stand alone PCs were installed in network versions on the LAN. These included WordStar 6.0 for word processing, SuperCalc 5.0 for spreadsheets and Picture Cardbox for small databases. Files which had been created by all these applications on stand alone PCs were easily transferred to the LAN file server.

DOBIS and STAIRS were made accessible on the LAN by fitting a token ring interface card into the IBM 9370 mainframe. The 3270 emulation software needed to enable PCs to emulate dumb terminals was loaded centrally on the file server. This initially linked to the mainframe via a PC running 3270 software as a gateway. This gateway was later removed so that LAN workstations now loaded 3270 emulation software from the file server and established a peer to peer communications session with the mainframe across the token ring. The mainframe was a true server on the LAN, and it was even possible to take down the file server without affecting someone already searching DOBIS or STAIRS. Most of the old dumb terminals used to access DOBIS and STAIRS were no longer needed and SDLC connections to ODA Library and other remote sites were unaffected.

The ISIS system could not be directly connected as a server on the LAN in the same way as the IBM mainframe because the architecture of the Plessey mini computer in use would not support the necessary network interface card. The solution adopted was to connect its serial ports to an asynchronous communications server on the LAN running Netware communications server software. The general communications package Crosstalk was then used to enable LAN workstations to emulate VT100 terminals when making calls to the communications server for connections to the ISIS system. In effect ISIS appeared to Netware as an independent external source delivering a number of asynchronous streams of data, rather than as a true server on the LAN. A similar arrangement was established to provide remote access to DTI Library's ISIS system from FCO, with a BT link interpolated between the communications server and DTI's ISIS system.

More recently the FCO ISIS database has been moved to a PC platform which is connected directly through a network interface card to the token ring. The ISIS application would not support the Netware IPX protocol and instead NETBIOS was used to support peer to peer communication sessions between the server and individual workstations on the token ring. FCO was the first site to implement this client server approach to networking ISIS on a PC LAN. This approach has an advantage over mapping asynchronous lines onto the LAN via a comms server in that there is no limit, other than the terms of the licence, to the number of workstations which can access the ISIS server concurrently.

The communications server was also used to provide connections to external online hosts, with the dial up details of individual hosts configured within Crosstalk. Four of the external ports on the communications server were set up with asynchronous connections to dedicated modems and BT lines. This meant that any workstation could be used to perform an online search up to a maximum of four simultaneous sessions. Available modems were pooled and allocated to meet requests for access to external sources using Netware's Asynchronous Services Interface software.

The effect of introducing the LAN was to integrate the diverse systems and applications which had been developed by the library during the 1980s. The token ring acted as the medium for communication and Netware acted as the glue which held the varoius components together. Netware's menu utility meant that technical details of establishing communications sessions between a workstation and any of the diverse servers and external systems could be neatly concealed from library staff. The various facilities available to each workstation on the LAN are presented through a unified, seamless interface.

In May 1992 the LAN was moved with the Cornwall House Library to a new site in the main FCO building in Whitehall. The two libraries amalgamated on this site and the LAN was upgraded and extended to support both this and a separate Legal Library. This completed the integration of FCO Library systems using the LAN to support about 40 workstations in five different locations in the main building. Netware was upgraded to the then latest version 3.11 and fibre optic cable was used to cover the considerable distances between library sites and offices within the building. A CD-ROM tower with four CD drives was connected to the file server to provide workstation access to the most frequently used CD-ROMs. Some LAN workstations also had local CD-ROM drives attached with applications software loaded locally. Initially Micro Design's SCSI Express product was used to network CD-ROMs, but a number of key CD-ROM applications did not run satisfactorily with this and it was replaced with Meridian Data's CD-Net. The growth in demand for networked CDs as a partial substitute for expensive online sources led to an expansion in the number of CD drives attached to the LAN from 4 to 21.

At the time of writing DOBIS/STAIRS and the IBM mainframe on which these appliations run are being replaced by SIRSI's Unicorn Collection Management system running under Unix on an IBM RS/6000. This downsizing is taking place because technological development has meant that it is no longer cost effective for the FCO to run integrated library and text retrieval systems on a mainframe platform under a proprietary environment. Moreover, the DOBIS/STAIRS applications are no longer formally supported by the original supplier. Unicorn offers enhanced functionality and is based on BRS Search which is part of the FCO standard software environment. Networking of Unicorn at FCO is supported by the TCP/IP protocol running on the LAN.

A variety of PCs have been used as LAN workstations ranging from diskless 286 machines with 1MB RAM to hard disk 486 machines with 8 MB RAM. This has raised a number of memory management problems and to some degree constrained the applications which could be run on certain workstations. The basic problem is that PCs need a variety of memory resident software to connect to the LAN and to communicate with the various servers on the network. This limits the amount of memory available for applications and can prevent them from running at all. A number of steps have been taken to minimise this problem. Firstly, as much as possible of the network driver software is loaded into expanded memory using the memory management facilities under DOS 5.0. This leaves as much conventional memory as possible free for applications. Secondly, a utility was installed to unload Netware's menus when they are not being displayed. This means that when an application is selected from a menu, instead of retaining the menu in memory while the application is running, a temporary file is created on disk which Netware uses to recreate the menu when the user exits from the application. Thirdly, all applications software in use was scrutinised for TSR (Terminate and Stay Resident) modules which are left in memory after the application has finished running. These can sometimes be unloaded without having to reboot the PC. These three expedients have largely solved the "RAM cram" problem though some switching of workstations is occasionally necessary to give the more powerful machines to users who make the heaviest demands.

The most demanding applications in use on the LAN are those running under Windows such as the desk top publishing package Aldus Pagemaker. Only eight of the more powerful PCs currently on the LAN are capable of supporting this satisfactorily and these are distributed to allow access for users with greatest requirements to use the package. Figure 2 is a simplified representation of the LAN.

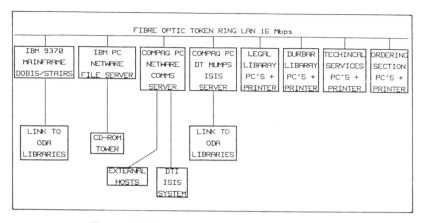

Figure 2: Integration Through Networking

Effects of Networking on Library and Information Services

The development of desktop access to the complete range of library systems has resulted in a major improvement to the information resources and tools available to library staff. This has in turn had a significant impact on the range and quality of library and information services delivered to end users. A number of specific benefits of networking can be identified:

1. *Ease of access to databases*: staff have had greater ease of access to the DOBIS/LIBIS library management system and the STAIRS text retrieval system which supports current awareness services and in house databases. Wider use of these resources has been visible both in the average number of users logged into these databases and in the overall utilisation of the IBM mainframe which supports them. Before the introduction of the LAN this IBM system was working below capacity, but it is now fully utilised without being overloaded. While increased use of the system is partly a function of increased demand for library services, it is also because staff do not need to move away from their desks to a dedicated workstation to search the library's main databases. Ease of access to library databases will be enhanced once the Unicorn system goes live, since the new system will contain all the data converted from DOBIS and STAIRS within a single application.

2. *Sharing of information resources*: the LAN has provided a means of sharing information and this has increased efficiency and extended access to a range of resources:

- Bibliographies are created by members of enquiry teams and stored online as documents in a shared directory. This avoids duplication of work and means that bibliographies can be easily located and updated.

- A networked database of enquiries has been established to avoid repetition of work in response to similar enquiries.

- Press cutting profiles for members of the FCO and its overseas posts are stored online in a shared directory which can be easily accessed and updated by library staff.

- A database containing scanned images of photographs in the library's historical photograph collection has been set up under Picture Cardbox.

- Word processing files can be transferred between different members of staff to avoid unnecessary printing out, rekeying and transfer by floppy disk. This is especially useful when seeking comments from colleagues on draft documents.

3. *Presentation of information*: the degree of integration of different packages afforded by the LAN means that staff can download searches from in house or external databases directly into their own directory. This means that editing the results of searches is straight forward and the quality of presentation has increased accordingly.

4. *Sharing of scarce hardware resources*: the availability of laser printers is a key factor in the quality of printed output. This is especially important at the FCO Library where many of the library users are in overseas Embassies and correspondence is the main form of communication. All correspondence is produced on one of six network laser printers which service some forty workstations.

5. *Efficient use of CD-ROM*: FCO Library makes substantial use of external online databases, and networking of CDs offers scope to make savings on the cost of online searches. In the case of newspapers a number of individual CDs are needed to cover the same volume of information as can be searched in one file or group of files on FT-Profile. The difficulty of finding the right CD, loading it in a drive and changing the CD several times during a search has acted as a deterrent to staff fully exploiting CDs on stand alone CD-ROM workstations. With networked CDs staff simply select the required CD from the menu at their workstation. This is likely to have an impact on the

balance of cd-rom and online resources used as staff take advantage of the cost saving potential of cds.

As more publications have become available on CD-ROM FCO departments outside the library have begun to request access to information in this format rather than traditional printed media, for example Hansard and Justis Parliament on cd-rom. Rather than purchasing individual copies of cds for each department wanting to use cds, the Library LAN has been extended to end users to provide them with access to a single copy of the cd mounted on the Library's cd server. This is part of the Library's wider approach to managing published information resources for the FCO as a whole including online and cd-rom access in end user departments, for which the Library holds the budget.

These various benefits of introducing a LAN have enabled a limited number of library staff to provide a more rapid and effective range of services at a time when dmand for the library's services has increased.

During the time the LAN has been in place the library has undergone a fundamental restructuring to enable staff to meet the requirements of users more closely. This restructuring has involved a move away from the traditional Reader Services/Technical Services divide. Most staff are now formed into five teams with responsibility for providing a complete range of library services to their own group of users. Users are allocated to library teams on a geographical basis with, for example, all British Embassies and other Posts in North and South America together with their corresponding Departments in the FCO in London allocated to one team. Library staff in the Americas Team deal with all enquiries from their users, select and initiate orders for publications on their behalf, catalogue books covering their geographical areas and market the library's services to their users.

The availability of a complete and integrated range of information systems to each member of the five teams is a prerequisite for the effective functioning of this type of library structure. To provide a complete range of services to their users, most library staff need desktop access to all of the library's systems: in house databases, external hosts, cd-roms, word processing etc. The distributed computing model implicit in the LAN both mirrors and supports the distributed staff structure which has been developed to deliver services to the FCO and its overseas posts. Without the LAN the evolution to a team based staff structure would have exacerbated the limitations of the diverse and discretely structured systems formerly in use to support a more traditional library structure.

Network Management Issues

The projects to install and upgrade the LAN were managed by a project manager from FCO's Information Systems Division working in conjunction with library systms staff, as is the current project to install Unicorn. All components of the library network are now managed by a Library Systems Manager on Librarian grade with some of the routine systems administration forming part of an Assistant Librarian's job. Continuity of staff in this area can be something of a problem, as Library staff moving into systems management work need a particular aptitude for dealing with IT, and it can take a considerable amount of time to develop the necessary experience and skills to make a full contribution. Demand for maintenance and development of library systems in recent years has tended to be constrained by the availability of suitably qualified and experienced staff. The LAN is entirely self contained within the library and does not impinge on any other FCO systems or networks other than those in the ODA. A number of suppliers are contracted to provide support for hardware and systems and applications software.

The complexity and variety of hardware, environments and applications which are integrated by the LAN means that library systems staff need a broad range of network and application management skills. For most of the standard products in use such as Netware and DOS based applications it is comparatively easy to develop these skills through a variety of external courses and hands on experience over a period of time. The substantial IT component of some courses at departments of library and information studies means that staff may have substantial formal training and experience of IT as applied to library and information management before moving into systems work. Two specialised areas which have taxed library systems staff are managing the IBM mainframe which runs a VSE/CICS/VTAM environment and trouble shooting communications problems with remote sites. These problems will be resolved by the imminent replacement of the proprietary IBM system with Unicorn, when Information Systems Division communications specialists will become more actively involved in managing links to remote sites.

Security and integrity of data on the library network are a major consideration. Storing all files on servers rather than on individual PCs means that backups of all data can be effectively managed by library systems staff. Individual library staff need not worry about backing up any of their files. As far as possible backups are carried out automatically during the night and a regime of cycling backups off site is in place. A virus test facility is used to scan any software being imported to the LAN from an external source. A number of workstations are fitted with contingency facilities which allow them to load software from local hard disks and to access DOBIS and STAIRS on the IBM mainframe even when the Netware file server is not running. This limits disruption to core library services when maintenance and development has to be carried out during prime user time.

One side effect of developing the LAN has been hardware obsolescence. Proprietary dumb terminals and dot matrix printers have been replaced by PCs acting as network workstations and networked laser printers. Existing PCs were converted to LAN workstations by installing network interface cards when the LAN was installed. As applications become more demanding both of memory requirements and processing power workstations need to be upgraded. Many of the LAN workstations are now out of date and are unable to support the many Windows based applications which have emerged in recent years. These older workstations are shortly to be replaced by PCs with 486/SX processors with 8MB RAM.

The LAN now forms a stable structure on which to develop existing and new applications. Token ring and Netware are well established as standards, and a wide choice of hardware and software is available to fit in with this environment. Individual applications and services available on the LAN can be upgraded or added to without affecting the structure or functioning of other components. After live running of the new Unicorn system, a number of specific developments are likely or possible in the near future:

(1) *Importing bibliographic records*: various CDs and external databases are being investigated as a source of bibliographic records to import into Unicorn. Whichever option is chosen all library staff involved in cataloging material will be able to search the CD or remote bibliographic database from their personal workstation.

(2) *Linking remote sites*: there are a number of remote FCO library sites which it is hoped to link into the main library network to enhance service provision. Some end users would also benefit from access to the OPAC in their offices.

(3) *E-mail:* E-mail exists within the DOBIS application but has not been extensively used because it does not alert users to new messages and it requires users to log into the DOBIS application to use it. The library would benefit from an E-mail system installed at the operating system level so that users would be alerted to new messages whatever package

45

they were using.

(4) *Fax server*: library staff regularly print out documents from the LAN and fax them to overseas Embassies and elsewhere. There is clear scope to introduce a fax server which would allow staff to fax documents directly from their workstations. Distribution of incoming faxes would also be enhanced.

(5) *Document Image Processing systems*: consideration has been given to using the LAN to support a Document Image Processing system. The library already holds a database of enquiries for Embassies, and one application of image processing would be to store scanned images of relevant documents along with the details of the enquiry.

(6) The Library is in the process of establishing dial up access to JANET and Internet from a single stand alone PC. This is being done on an experimental basis in the first instance, but there is a possibility of extending access to all workstations on the LAN if the experiment is successful.

The rapidly evolving role of library and information services in government libraries and elsewhere is partially driven by technological development. A key element of this development is the use of networking technology to integrate diverse systems and to extend access to an ever increasing range of electronic information. The provision of desktop, workstation access to a wide range of information resources, as seen in the FCO Library, reflects a progression towards a more user-centred approach to information systems, where the network workstation becomes the user's gateway to the information world. As networking within and between organisations expands the traditional role of library and information services will continue to evolve in parallel. Traditional activities such as cataloguing will become increasingly obsolete, to be superseded by new activities and roles of managing and coordinating networked, electronic information resources and the tools to exploit them. De facto and OSI based networking standards are likely to play an important part as the expansion of networking and the transformation it brings to library and information services accelerates during the 1990s.

Use of Local Area Network Technology in an Information-Oriented Organization

Pablo Dubois
International Coffee Organization

This article presents a succinct account of an operational Local Area Network that is central to the working methods of a small organisation where information collection, storage and dissemination are key areas. The International Coffee Organization (ICO) is an intergovernmental organisation established to administer the International Coffee Agreement, an international treaty designed to achieve a reasonable balance between world supply and demand for coffee.[1] The Organization has some 60 Member countries and has headquarters in London with a current staff of 43.

Until July 1989 the Organization administered a price stabilization scheme for coffee based on a system of export quotas. Following a failure on the part of Members to agree on the renewal of this mechanism the Organization has continued to function as a forum for the discussion of problems affecting the world coffee economy, as a source of detailed statistical data on coffee designed to aid Members in analysing and formulating decisions, and as a general source of information on coffee. There are at least 50 significant coffee-producing countries and consumption is a global phenomenon. The economic importance of coffee to producing countries is high; not only is it an important source of export earnings, but in many cases it is the primary source, with several countries depending on coffee for over 50 per cent of total export revenues. In importing countries coffee is one of the most widely traded and advertised consumer products.

It follows therefore that the Organization is geared to receiving, processing and disseminating large volumes of information, with emphasis on communications, storage and retrieval, analytic tools, dissemination technology and, increasingly, electronic publishing. Apart from the Office of the Executive Director the structure of the Organization consists of:

- Secretariat Services with a staff of 16, divided into Units covering Information (Library and Intelligence), Translation (four official languages are recognized), Document production and Printing;

- Statistical Services, including an Economic Adviser and two Units responsible for Exports, Imports and Prices, and Supply and Certificates respectively;

- Administrative Services, comprising Units responsible for Accounts, Personnel/Office Management and Computer systems administration.

The Organization has used various data processing technologies for storing and retrieving data from Certificates of Origin since the early 1970s, and transferred these operations in-house in 1979/80. In 1988 a decision was taken to standardise where possible on PC-compatible systems and, at the end of 1989, a Novell Netware LAN was commissioned. The system introduced at this stage has been progressively upgraded, particularly with regard to the introduction of Microsoft Windows in 1992. The current system is described below.

Hardware and physical layout: The Organization occupies four floors of which one is devoted to meeting rooms and reception areas and one to storage and coffee bar facilities. The accommodation is cabled throughout using Ethernet. The core of the Network is the File Server, a 64 Mb. Tandon Tower 486/33 EISA bus processor with 2.5 Gigabytes (duplexed) of central storage. All staff have full-time access to networked PCs. These comprise 35 Tandon 486s with 200 Mb hard discs, of which 13 have Philips 1710 17" Monitors, and 20 Tandon 386sx machines with 30 Mb removable Data Packs. A number of the latter are used as Print and Communications controllers. All networked PCs have 16 Bit Network interface cards. In addition a 64 Mb Sun Sparc Station 10 Model 30 with 1.3 Gigabyte storage and a Storage Dimensions Tahiti 2 Optical Erasable Subsystem are used to deal with Certificate data and image files, with the Sun attached to the Network. Printing equipment comprises 10 PostScript laser printers, and 5 24-pin and 15 8-pin dot matrix printers. Security backup is effected by a 4 millimetre Archive Python DAT unit and a 5 Gigabyte Exobyte cartridge unit. Three CD-ROM drives (Toshiba and Panasonic) are available but not networked. Finally the Organization has a number of scanners and a Philips CDD 521 Compact Disc Recorder.

The Network is based on the Novell Netware 3.11 system, with Windows 3.1 as a standard interface for most users. However in some areas, such as statistics, MS-DOS 5 continues in use.

Applications: In view of the international scope of the work of the Organization emphasis has been placed as a matter of policy on using industry-standard systems. Additionally considerable importance is given to compatibility between different applications packages. These can be divided into core applications, network applications and specialist applications.

Core applications—Communications: The Network uses Lotus cc:Mail as an internal messaging system and for internal file transfer. In addition the system has interfaced with General Electric Information Services (GEIS) Quik-Comm international electronic mail service for communications with a number of countries and agents. External addresses are integrated into the standard cc:Mail directory.

Core applications—Relational databases: Since 1993, Microsoft Access has been used as the main relational database tool by the Organization. It is used for a variety of purposes, some of which are listed below:

Computer hardware listing	Membership data
Computer software listing	Personnel records
Documents in progress (Transactional)	Press contacts
Events chronology	Software licences
Interpreters listing	Translators listing

Of particular interest is its use as a system for recording details of journals received by the Organization and as a tool for logging information enquiries. It is well suited for transactional databases and is used during periods of meetings of the Organization's Council or Executive Board to monitor the process of document creation and publishing.

Core applications—Word Processing: WordPerfect 5.2 (and WordPerfect 6.0 for Windows) is used for word processing throughout the

Organization and is the basic medium for document and publications creation into which material derived from other applications is integrated. For additional presentation facilities use is made of Aldus PageMaker 4.0.

Network applications—Text Management: Text retrieval is effected with the Personal Librarian version 3 package. A number of databases are available ranging from the basic bibliographical database system created by the Library and made available as the public Coffeeline (File 164 on Dialog) service, to full text databases comprising historical decisions and resolutions of the Organization's Council and Executive Board. All current documents of the Organization are currently being processed for access by this system. One feature of the system is that documents may be incorporated either in ASCII format or retained in WordPerfect or Word. There is no need to duplicate documents for input purposes once they have been created in these formats. The system merely creates inverted files for retrieval purposes from the existing records.

An interesting feature of Personal Librarian is the availability of ranked output from natural language formulations as well as conventional Boolean searching. In effect purely natural language formulations can be used for searching both unstructured and structured databases. In general the use of field tags and Boolean operators provides greater precision where data is structured into fields. Nevertheless the ranking system, by providing a bar chart display to illustrate degrees of relevance over the range of records retrieved, is the preferred retrieval mode for full text databases and gives good results for structured bibliogaphical databases as well.

As a Windows product Personal Librarian allows text from displayed records to be selected and copied to the Clipboard for incorporation into new documents. This is an effective working tool since it is easy to minimise one application when copying retrieved data into another. A further useful feature is the existence of hypertext linking to attach or cross refer to relevant files, many of which may be in different applications. For instance a full text WordPerfect document may contain tables which are best held as separate files accessible through hypertext linking rather than being put through a largely meaningless indexing process. Hypertext links are effective too for access to image files (a number of TIF files derived from colour scanned images are held) and graphs (usually in Lotus).

Network applications—Spreadsheets: Lotus 1-2-3 for Windows is used for applications requiring spreadsheet technology, particularly in the following areas: accounts, graphical presentation of statistics, and external dissemination of statistical data. Lotus files can be incorporated into WordPerfect documents where needed.

Specialist applications—Statistics: Statistical data on coffee is notoriously complex in view of the number of countries and specific time series involved. All statistics are handled in the Organization through Information Resources' Express system, which provides a variety of validation, storage, computation and report generation facilities. However there is a limitation on the number of available software licences for this product, and output is typically generated in the Statistical units as report files for further use in documents, or in some cases in spreadsheet format.

Specialist applications—Graphics: Harvard Graphics is used for tasks requiring certain types of graphical output. In some areas where images have been scanned into the system they are held in the Photofinish or Paintshop systems.

Specialist applications—Scanning: Scanning is divided into OCR and image scanning. The former uses Omnipage 2 for conversion of scanned text to WordPerfect; the latter mainly uses the Trimco Wintrack Document Image Processing system. In the case of Omnipage-scanned documents these are usually accessed subsequently through Personal Librarian, whereas the images scanned using Trimco are retrieved using Wintrack software which allows retrieval by field values and keywords. Wintrack is in fact available through the Network on 5 PCs. The choice of technique is dependent here on three factors:

- Access requirements: for archival material wide access is not necessary;

- Quality of the original: OCR scanning is most effective where good quality original text exists, thereby avoiding time-consuming editing; apart from allowing retrieval via a full text management system text files occupy far less space than image files;

- Volume of material: the Trimco DIP system allows a more rapid process of scanning and incorporation into a database.

Specialist applications—external database searching: Links to external databases are not directly available to most networked PCs. In part this is a reflection of lack of demand from the majority of staff but the need to control costs is also a factor. Nevertheless downloaded search results are easily circulated to users via the Network.

A Network Administrator is responsible for maintenance, trouble-shooting and configuration, assisted by a System Support Administrator. However, the investigation and introduction of new systems and applications has also required the regular use of external consultancy.

The implementation of LAN applications in the Organization has had considerable impact in terms of a general process of re-engineering administrative structures since the late 1980s. By introducing common working tools and an overall framework of communication throughout the Organization, the process of developing flatter management structures and the formation of ad hoc Project Groups for particular tasks has been greatly enhanced. The documentation of working procedures in the various areas of work of the Organization is currently being consolidated. Procedures are in all cases directly associated with job descriptions and network applications. It is significant that a number of new products and services are under consideration, and when developed should allow some quantification of productivity gains compared with the pre-LAN period.

An important aspect of working in a LAN environment is the development of standards for file and directory nomenclature. The initial approach in the Organization was to encourage the development of subdirectories and file names which were as transparent as possible, avoiding coding systems intelligible only to limited numbers of people. These guidelines have in practice worked quite well although efforts are now being made to introduce a more systematic apprcach. This involves the retention of transparent directory and subdirectory names (eg CERTS for Certificates) with two letter codes for filename components. The latter would include two subject codes, an individual code, a version number and an application file extension code. Thus a file dealing with the transmission of certificates from Brazil could be placed in a subdirectory entitled CERTS and be called CEBRIC05.wp where BR is the ISO country code, IC refers to the file's original author, 05 is the reference number designating a particular file created by the same author on the same topic and .wp an indicator that the file is a WordPerfect file.

The use of the Network has a positive impact on the contribution made by the role of Library and Information services in three areas:

- the services are integrated into the operational framework of the Organization;

- enquiry answering is speeded up and material (eg search results can be supplied easily in machine-readable form);

- Current awareness facilities are improved. Material can either be circulated to specific users via electronic mail or placed in Bulletin Boards. The latter can be done without recourse to a specialised mail system simply by placing material in a designated general access directory on the File Server.

Implementation and training: It is not possible to generalise on these aspects since the successful implementation of a LAN is linked to the existing level of IT familiarity in any Organization. However given the need for careful systems configuration, standards, a wider familiarity with applications, and quality monitoring, the time required should not be underestimated and should be computed in months rather than weeks for an application of the size described.

References

1. International Coffee Organisation: *International Coffee Agreement 1983*. (Article 1.) International Coffee Organisation, 1982.

Networking in the Department of the Environment

John Scott-Cree

Department of the Environment

Approximately ten years ago, the Department of the Environment installed a data communications network (DCN). It originally served approximately 200 departmental computer bureau users and by early 1993 it was serving over 3000 users in DOE and DOT. However, the DCN is relatively expensive, costing over £1.5 million per annum, and is technically incapable of enhancement to support future requirements including the Advanced Office Support System (AOSS) project. It is based upon a number of leased lines connecting statistical multiplexors to form an intelligent switched network.

There is a perceived strategic need to maximise the effectiveness of the Department's IT investment by inter-connecting computer resources at three levels:

- at the *desktop* (PCs), connected locally to . . .

- *business area* processors (usually called Local Area Network (LAN) servers), connected by Wide Area Network (WAN) to . . .

- *corporate* facilities (eg bureau services, EMail, AOSS).

The strategic objective is to provide networking which supports:

- the geographically dispersed nature of the Department;
- the increasing trend toward using local and distributed computing resources.

Implementation of the strategy within the Department needs to take account of the following constraints:

- variations in the pace and diversity of requirements in the different business areas;
- uncertainties which remain over the relocation of the London estate;
- uncertainties over the likely pace and scope of the AOSS project
- tight public sector expenditure constraints.

Forecasting levels of demand and the timing of the provision is difficult, and the Department needs to fund work from within existing allocations. A single, comprehensive or "Big Bang" implementation of new networks could not be justified. Instead, an approach satisfying the following criteria is necessary:

- *incremental* but based on standards which ensure future compatibility and provide flexibility;
- plans to be *modular* and *independent* (ie each step should provide services in its own right and overall plans should not hinge on provisions in any one building);
- each implementation step should be *cost-justified* in its own right.

Two broad initiatives would proceed in parallel.

- *At the tactical level*, on a cost replacement basis to put in place over one to two years a base infrastructure, and to provide electronic office facilities such as electronic mail.
- *At the strategic level*, to address the long term requirements and the provision of telecommunications services in the new London HQ office(s). The Strategic WAN Project is assessing the need for WAN connectivity across

the department, with a view to commencing implementations by the end of the financial year. This may include, potentially, the use of managed services.

It is envisaged that by adopting this approach, projects such as AOSS and the Accounting Systems Project (ASP) would be provided with a working infrastructure which has already been cost justified, and thereby reduce the new investment costs which they would individually need to justify.

In December 1992 under the Network Infrastructure Procurement (NIP) project, a contract was awarded to ICL to provide the Department with a flexible and compatible set of telecommunications products. These include:

- ICL DRS 6000 Series processors running under NX UNIX to act as LAN servers using Portable Netware;

- structured cabling using unshielded twisted pair and a variety of 10 Base T equipment;

- server based versions of standard application software.

Using the NIP contract a Departmental project team was established to implement networks at the tactical level. This resulted in an initial programme of work to provide data cabling in most of the Regional Offices, and a partial provision in Marsham Street and other HQ buildings.

Examples of Implementations

Office Services Division of which the Library is part, runs six LANs including Accommodation Services; Design Printing and Reprographics; Publication Sales Unit; and Business Machinery. There is a main financial system with a couple of smaller systems dealing with training and staff-in-post returns.

Prior to LAN installation, montly reports were compiled from floppy diskettes circulated to each branch for completion, with consequent delays as staff waited for a specific machine to become free before being able to verify information and enter data. Individual staff were required to take regular and frequent back-ups, but this relied on the machine being free from other users. There were no means of ensuring this and there was the possibility of gaps in back-ups which could cause difficulties if a hard disk became corrupt.

The LANs give management re-assurance that centralised back-ups of important data are made frequently and correctly. There are savings of staff time in backing-up their own data, and reduced waiting time in accessing shared data files. Rather than buy extra printers to meet demand, existing printers can be used by anybody on the LAN. There is the ability to mail electronically other members of the LAN.

Translation Service has a LAN comprising five PCs connected to a file server and two laser printers were installed in July 1990. The system was designed and set up by two consultants to cater for the rather specialised requirements of a small translation unit (a self-contained section of DOE Library). Each of the five translators was to have an individual PC providing word-processing facilities and access to a number of specially designed databases (using Cardbox Plus) containing records of specialist terminology, jobs and of a panel of freelance translators, as well as to communications and spreadsheet facilities.

Implementation of the facilities has taken place in stages and development is still underway. With the introduction of charging regimes in the Library, a further PC was added to develop the jobs record to provide costs information. Increasing demands in this area, however, have forced consideration of upgrading to a more sophisticated database. Other developments in prospect are:

- in the area of terminology, to enable the print-out of glossaries from the terminology database;
- communications, to enable the receipt and transmission of material via modem.

Library The DOE Library is based in Marsham Street where there is a segmentation of the infrastructure cabling which is made necessary because of the size of the office area on the Podium. The accommodation housing the Library staff who will use the LAN is contained in different cabling segments. This means that three patch panels and hubs will be required to make a single business area LAN. Current proposals suggest that the patch panel/hub domain will be linked by thin-wire Ethernet. A decision whether or not to use fibre optic links as an alternative will be made in the light of budgetary constraints.

Drinking Water Inspectorate (DWI): This was set up in January 1990. In order to check that water companies supply water which is safe to drink and which meets the stringent standards set in the Water Quality Regulations, the Inspectorate has to inspect, assess and process very large quantities of information. When DWI was set up it was decided that extensive implementation of IT would be required to handle this information.

DWI implemented IT in phases. The first phase involved individual PCs with word processing, spreadsheet and database applications to meet the immediate requirements of the section. This stand alone personal computer set up was not considered to meet fully the IT requirements of DWI.

The second phase was to implement a LAN. The 28 PCs connected to this network allow the users to:

- share hardware, for example laser printers, hard disks and memory;

- share software like DrawPerfect and Lotus which are not required by all members of the section;

- share files and databases;

- transfer files and data to other users using the LAN;

- provide electronic mail facility to send messages and documents;

- provide a central back-up facility.

DWI are currently carrying out additional configuration work on the LAN which will result in further benefits to the section.

Housing Right To Buy is situated in the North Tower of Marsham Street. This is a small business area LAN implementation linking 13 PC users with a shared printing resource.

West Midland Regional Office (WMRO) is based in Five Ways House, Birmingham. The initial implementation is for the LAN supporting 14 PC users in the Housing Casework work group. However the installed Server and network equipment has sufficient capacity to enable the planned extension of LAN services to

- the 4 PC user IT section;

- the 8 PC user European Branch;

- taking over the existing 16 PC user LAN.

Some 25 LANs have now been installed in various business areas.

LAN Joys and Miseries: a report from MAFF's Translators

Douglas d'Enno

Chief Translator, Ministry of Agriculture, Fisheries and Food

The Translation Section of the Ministry of Agriculture, Fisheries and Food has been in existence for over twenty years and in that time has translated, or arranged for the translation of, texts covering every sphere of the Ministry's activities, from aphid control to health requirements for the import of zoo animals into France. The section was originally part of EC Division but transferred to Main Library in early 1973. In the previous year the present complement of five translator posts was approved. Although the mainstay of the unit was originally the translation of texts from Brussels, there has been a gradual shift towards other areas of work, for example the translation of horticultural research papers from Dutch; indeed, this language, together with French and German, has for many years accounted for the bulk of the Section's output.

The benefits of computerisation (or at least wordprocessing, initially) were evident from the very outset. In 1982, we arranged for the demonstration of a new wordprocessor only to receive an official reprimand both from the unions and the Superintendent of Typists.

In retrospect, disputes with the unions effectively delayed the introduction of any kind of LAN system for some three years. After a lengthy campaign—and it was nothing less than that—we finally obtained the first local area network in the summer of 1987. We believe that this was in fact the first LAN to be supplied to any Ministry of Agriculture office. The set-up consisted of 3 IBM machines joined by a hideously thick and inflexible cable with a small pin at one end which was very liable to bend or snap off if removed from the PC for any reason. Apart from being unsightly, the cabling was something of a safety hazard even when tucked around the walls.

The first word processing package we were given by the Ministry was Samna IV, which had a persistent tendency to lock up and lose one's work. At the time, Smart software looked like a good replacement option but although it was officially approved we were later to sidestep it for WordPerfect.

The database we were running was Cardbox-Plus, which has served us well to this day. Initially, we did not have a network version annd simply operated single copies.

By and large, the network ran satisfactorily and even though the dot matrix output from that time looks rather substandard today it was a vast improvement over the handwritten text which had previously been the norm. The IBM Proprinter was a good example of how big such equipment could be; being a noisy machine, it required a hood and then took up even more space in the office.

The first phase in the unit's use of a LAN came to an end in April 1991, shortly after we had moved offices from 10 Whitehall Place to 3 Whitehall Place next door. The new premises were larger and the new equipment with which we were supplied (both software and hardware) was very much the latest thing: Compaq 386 machines, a scanner, a laser printer and, before long, a fax machine.

By that time, we had acquired a network version of Cardbox which has been found to be very reliable, although it does not react kindly to any irregular exit from the program. The commands needed to re-open the database are rather complicated and we have now simplified this into a batch file. Support from the distributors, Business Simulations, has always been excellent.

We also installed WordPerfect 5.1 (network version) and this too has served us well. There have occasionally been printer problems but these have been due more to the Novell Netware set-up rather than to the program itself.

Later in the year, we purchased Ashton-Tate's Rapidfile to be used as an "automatic ledger". Although not a network product, the program has enabled us to produce all kinds of statistics and to operate both freelance and in-house ledgers far more efficiently than was the case with paper ledgers. Naturally, printouts of any combinations of fields can easily be produced but in practice the data has remained firmly within the PC's. There is a disadvantage with Rapidfile, namely that only one person can have "operating rights" over the system at any one time; to avoid any overwrites or other clashes, the currently authorised operator keeps the backup floppy disk on his/her desk so that it is not available to other would-be users until he/she has finished. A rather primitive system, perhaps, but it does seem to work. Another aspect of Rapidfile which can be a disadvantage is the fact that only one file (ie one financial year) can be open at once, although with Windows it is possible to open another file or files via DOS.

Overall, when the LAN is working properly it can be very efficient. With the use of a program like Magellan, any key word can be found across the whole system within a matter of seconds. Cardbox-Plus has proved to be very effective and there can be no doubt that a translator's terminology collection does need to be on a network for optimum use, even within a small section. We tried and abandoned a couple of other systems (eg Termex) which in 1989 were not network-friendly.

One of the biggest disadvantages of LANs is the sheer complexity of the system, especially nowadays, so that we are very much in the hands of the suppliers and maintenance engineers. In our own case, the original installation was far from perfect due to having been hurried and it was many weeks before we were able to run it to our entire satisfaction. Since the new system was installed, we have had a procession of engineers from the maintenance company and very few of them have been really competent. Despite repeated pleas, we have never been able to get the original installing engineer back to clear up any problems we might have had. Within the last year, one of the LAN problems was the quality of maintenance and the terms on which it was being supplied.

A major headache in recent months has been the perennial problem of printer sharing; this has now been resolved, although we have found with our network that faults can develop spontaneously within the system which cannot be explained even by experienced maintenance engineers.

There is no question that problems can also arise whenever an upgrade of any kind is attempted. For example, the new version of DOS which one installs is almost sure not to co-exist happily with one software program or another and we have found the same difficulties with memory managers. Getting all the programs to live in harmony is something of an achievement within an office—we know from experience that the road can be a hard one.

Other mystery problems arise for which the only solution seems to be an upgrade (then other problems will arise). For example, our scanning software (Caere Omnipage) now refuses to run properly and an engineer's visit is needed. This could cost as much as £500, which is more than the value of the product itself. When we do upgrade, we are sure that the new program will hit some snag or other . . .

Although we have acquired one 486 machine, our other Compaqs are certainly beginning to show their age. The Ministry's Animal Health Division needs us to change over to Word for Windows 6 for the production of certificates; this is a very demanding package in terms of disk space, memory, etc, as far as we can see and does seem very slow in operation. Already, we have hit problems in getting bought-in foreign language fonts (Worldfont for Windows) to work with the system. In addition, network disk space usage is running very high, even without any new packages on board.

We are hoping that with the introduction of MAIDEN, the Ministry-wide strategic office automation system, we will be able to move into a faster and more efficient operating environment. This changeover is expected to take place this summer and we look forward to this development with interest and, in the time-honoured phrase, cautious optimism.

Printed in the United Kingdom for HMSO
Dd297911 10/94 C15 G55 10170

The Circle of State Librarians

Government library and information services operate in a rapidly changing environment where new technology and fresh demands have an impact on staff at all levels. CSL helps people in government service and related areas to keep abreast of new developments and to keep in touch with colleagues in other departments.

CSL aims to stimulate a common interest in the cost effective management of information, and to promote co-operation among staff in government and allied library and information services.

Full membership is open to all staff employed in UK government departments, and Associate membership to other's interested in the Circle's aims.

For more information please contact the following:

Chair: Mrs E MacLachlan, DTI, Room 116, 123 Victoria Street, London SW1E 6RB   Tel: 071-215 6697

Secretary: Mr K Jackson, CVL, New Haw, Addlestone, Surrey KT15 3NB   Tel: 0932 357603
